Married

MW00948415

The Blessing of Having Heaven At Home, Overcoming loss, and The Words That Could Save YOUR Marriage

Married to an M.G.T.

The Blessing of Having Heaven At Home, Overcoming loss, and The Words That Could Save YOUR Marriage

Jihad Hassan Muhammad
Rodney 'Asaad' Muhammad

© 2014 MASQ Media Group

© 2014 MASQ Media Group
All World-Wide Rights Reserved
Printed in the United States of America.

ISBN-13: 978-1499539691
ISBN-10: 149953969X

This publication may not be reproduced, stored in a retrieval system, or transmitted in whole or in part, in any form or by any means, electronic, mechanical, photocopying, recording, or otherwise, without the prior written permission of MASQ Media Group.

MASQ Media Group (www.MarriedToAnMGT.com)
P.O. Box 18382, Phoenix, AZ 85005
(323) 533-6132

TABLE OF CONTENTS

Haziqah Safiyah Muhammad

Tonja Rene Muhammad

Introduction The Therapy, The Black Woman and The Purpose - Jihad

"The strength of a thing is measured by its ability to withstand great force or pressure."
-The Hon. Min. Louis Farrakhan

As March 10, 2014 came my family and I were struck with a staggering blow, a blow that some never recover from. This blow was the blow of death. My friend and beloved wife had passed, her physical form just existed as a shell now, and she was no longer alive in that form. I would never hold her again. I would never pray with her again, as we loved to start our day doing. I would never be able to have a long conversation with her about how if our community would just accept this life giving teaching from The Most Hon. Elijah Muhammad, and the work that his extension in The Hon. Min. Louis Farrakhan is doing; we could save ourselves from the drugs, crime, poverty, sex without responsibility, and so forth that has us facing incarceration, death, HIV/AIDS, the destruction of our families, and more, as she and I would talk for hours about. The children would never see their mother again. They would never feel her comfort, her soft kiss, her gentle hugs and encouragement, her cooking their favorite meals, and sewing them their garments, all that was over now. Her beloved mother had lost a daughter she gave birth to, and held, since she was her beautiful baby, and showered with love as she continued to do when my wife became an adult. All of this was over for family and friends...Stephanie Patrice Muhammad as many knew her, and more recently under the name Haziqah Safiyah Muhammad, was no more to grace us with her physical presence.

We had faith that she would overcome this recent condition as she was in the hospital just over a week for a blood clot that suddenly developed in her brain. Our faith was undying and unmoving, and she began to show great progress, yet man plans and Allah (God) plans, and He is the best of planners.

The staggering blow was coupled with the fact that she was 10 weeks pregnant, and as she was in the hospital I was graced to see the baby in the womb, which despite her condition the baby was healthy, with as the doctors said, "a strong heart beat," as I saw him or her moving around. I began to focus through this great pain of which I have never felt before, and say I cannot succumb, I must fight through, I must stay among the living, and accept God's will. I began to focus on life and Haziqah's legacy, and how she will live forever.

What is life, and what is death? Life by definition is said to be a process of a living organism. Biological processes are made up of any number of chemical reactions or other events that result in a transformation. Death is defined as a cessation of these processes. The Hon. Minister Louis Farrakhan teaches us that life activity is to engage in that which brings forth a transformation in the lives of our families, neighborhoods, community, and world, and with the cessation of this activity, we can be considered dead. I prayed to continue to engage in life activity, particularly as it relates to our youth, since their lives are being taken at a rapid pace.

I was already on a journey with a program my brother in Islam, James W. Muhammad and I founded called Dynasty Hip-Hop Mentoring Program. Its work is what I feel is the fulfillment of what The Hon. Min. Louis Farrakhan has taught the hip-hop community in regards to accepting the responsibility to lead our youth, and the power hip-hop has to affect our youth over most things. So with this program we were able to get youth off the streets and out of gangs, and be more productive. My wife was a great help to me on this journey. She had great love for our brothers and sisters on the streets and was fearless in expressing it to them. So I began to work hard to increase my efforts with the program because it increased life activity. It helped to keep what Haziqah represented alive.

Since her passing at the dinner table, the children and I daily keep the memory of her by talking about the good times had with her; this has been a great help for them.

Allah had other plans, other aspects of His mathematics, for His purpose. Those plans developed with another death. My brother in Islam, Rodney Assad Muhammad, was struck with this same death blow, not even a month after the loss of my wife. I learned through Dr. Wesley Muhammad that our brother was in the throes of this same great trial. So I reached out to my brother Rodney, even though I had never met him. I had to support him, Allah (God) moved me to. I felt I could be a help to him since I was walking a little further down the same road he was just beginning. This was why we have a brotherhood! I thought to myself. The brotherhood, the Fruit of Islam, which Allah (God) himself in the Person of Master Fard Muhammad came and set up so that we as Black men could return back to who we were before our destruction which made us into slaves by an open enemy. The Most Hon. Elijah Muhammad's work in building this brotherhood, and the Hon. Minister Louis Farrakhan's continued efforts in making us better men, husbands, fathers, sons, and brothers is what makes the brotherhood strong. I had to be a brother to Rodney. I called him and he received me with open arms. Oft times when people go through the pain of death they shut others out, especially others they may not know. He opened up that I might be able to help him, and he became a help to me during this rough period of our lives.

It is because of this brotherhood that two Black men who have never met each other, one on the west coast, and one in the southwest, have begun to check on each other and see if each other are alright, becoming a support during this most difficult time. Helping one another get through the loss of two strong and loving Black women that were gracious women of respect in the Muslim Girls in Training (M.G.T.) and General Civilization Class (G.C.C.) in the Nation of Islam.

As Rodney and I talked daily we began to share our experiences with the community on social media, and many were inspired. This was therapeutic for us. So my brother Rodney said, "Let's share this with the world, and write a book." Since we have been writing about our pain, he wanted to help the people. Our words began to make them reflect with an overwhelming response. And with every thought I share, with every word I write, I feel so much better in helping others get through their pain, and bear witness to what they have in their spouse, and family, because we are an example that you could lose them at any moment.

We are fighting through it all, feeling that Allah (God) backs us in our efforts of good. Pain is necessary, and hard trials are necessary to establish truth.

Our sister Tonja Muhammad; my brother Rodney's wife, and my wife Haziqah gave their lives daily to see Black Women raised from the bowels of disrespect to the standard of goddesses...which they showed and proved as students in the M.G.T.- G.C.C., that they loved so intensely. The world must know that there is a man in The Hon. Min. Louis Farrakhan that is redeeming Black women utilizing this training called the M.G.T. It is the solution to what America has made out of our women since slavery. America has made bitches, ho's, sluts, whores, jump offs, and all manner of other names and actions of disrespect out of Black women in particularly, and of all oppressed women.

She is now a standard of everything the world once considered unmentionable by way of reality TV, radio, and mass media. The M.G.T. is the answer to that problem. She is the standard of respect, extreme and uncontested beauty, and divinity, so much so that even our brothers in the streets who because of the culture of disrespect of Black women, usually show none, yet with the M.G.T. they bow and give respect because they see what she displays.

Our wives represented that daily, we must tell the world the prize of being married to women like these, and how it is a solution to the ills that currently threaten the families in our community.

The journey of death continues to show us that we must love and enjoy each other NOW; for we do not know when the hour will come that we will not be able to do so. Even if there are disputes among us, we must get to the root of the dispute and solve it quickly so that the spirit of love and unity is present. The Most Hon. Elijah Muhammad says, and the Hon. Minister Louis Farrakhan shows through his example, that we must force unity.

We pray this book might save some marriages and mend some families...STAY TUNED

Introduction Healing In His Wings - Asaad

There is healing in His wings! (Malachi 4:2)

In writing this book there is a feeling of relief from the grief. Some that I have spoken to since the transition of my wife Tonja Rene Muhammad on April 8, 2014 have expected me to be grief stricken, despondent and numb due to what has happened. My wife was enjoying life and in attendance at her M.G.T. - G.C. Class on Saturday the April 5th, decided to stay home from the Sunday meeting to prepare for an outing with some sisters at a Native American POW WOW. She left home at 2pm in high spirits and ready to enjoy her sisterhood time and by 6pm I had gotten a call that she fell ill from "something she ate." By Tuesday morning she was being rushed to the emergency room and by Tuesday afternoon April 8th while waiting on an emergency flight in my attempt to get to her side, I received the call that would forever change the course of what I thought was my destiny. I was told by one of my wife's closest friends who was by her side that "she didn't make it..." Yes there is sadness and pain however I am also full of life and happiness due to a knowingness of the power of Allah (God). I have been blessed with large amounts of creative energy since I was a child and I always found solace in art, music and song. However this life altering event has unlocked something deeper within me. I am recognizing it as the hand of Allah (God) bringing forth my true purpose. I have always served and helped others. My mother used to bring broken VCR machines home from co-workers just for me to fix. I watched as my mother cared for children that were not her own, some of whom came directly from their mothers' wombs into my mother's arms and she cared for them through adulthood. So service has been in my life and environment and has also been my greatest struggle.

You have heard the saying "...to whom much is given, much is required..." (Luke 12:48). I have found that all the times I attempted to run from service and run from helping, my life, soul and mind would never be at ease. Writing this book has allowed me to complete three missions: One to do what my wife was trying to encourage me to do the week before her transition, which was to increase my level of service to our Nation and community using the gifts and talents Allah has deposited within me. Two to serve and save a fallen people and most importantly third to finally submit to what Allah (God) wants from me. The day my wife transitioned my sadness was not solely because of the person no longer physically present but for who she was at her core. I no longer had my helpmeet, friend, lover, companion, mirror holder, chef, consoler, business partner, etc. My desire to (and many days I do) scream loudly is my attempt to tell the world of her VALUE, my tears are tears of joy over the BLESSING she is. A Muslim Girl in Training (M.G.T.) is a blessed thing and everyone deserved to know about it.

When Allah (God) revealed (through 7 phone calls) the first phase of His purpose for my life as it relates to this, I knew it was not just *my* journey but *our* journey together.

Sharing this experience online was in my mind just a modern way of the grieving process, however Allah (God) being the best of planners, He gave life where there was talk of death. As a product of adultery, abuse in the home and dysfunctional family structures, Allah revealed to me that it was my mission to help in the mighty work of healing marriages and families. So as I said to my Allah (God) while in deep prayer on the night of my wife's transition: "Here I am Allah (God), use me!" And He answered in multiple ways one of which was a destiny phone call from brother Jihad Hassan Muhammad whom I had never personally met before this, but we would share a kindred experience and near identical blessing in the women we were honored to call our wives. I pray that Allah (God) guides my and our hand and you find hope, faith and healing within these pages as I attempt to hear and obey Allah (God) that was coming through the voice of my wife...the journey begins and continues...

"The Honorable Elijah Muhammad said that, 'Seventy five percent of His work was with the female.' Therefore, He strived mightily to make something of the Black woman. He taught her how to sew and cook, how to rear her children, how to take care of her husband, how to keep a clean home, and in general He taught her how to act at home and abroad. His desire was to produce a very high level of civilization coming through a reformed female. He took great joy in seeing our women come from a low state or condition constantly improving themselves. He taught them about loud raucous behavior and laughter. He loved to hear the refined speech of the female. He wanted her highly educated, cultivated, and refined. He taught the female how to walk, sit and stand. He showed her, her mother's dressing room that she had not seen in 400 years; meaning He showed her the styles of the righteous women of the East from whom she is a descendant. He loved to see her speaking with firmness to men and never being forward in the presence of men. He hated sisters to speak to men with soft, sultry speech. He taught her, as well as the male, according to the Qur'an that both should lower their gaze when they are in each other's company. He dressed the female in such a way that men could not know the beauty of their form, but, would only become acquainted with the beauty of their faces and their expressions so that the male would not be physically attracted to her alone, but, spiritually attracted to her as well."

- The Honorable Minister Louis Farrakhan, "Men of this World do not Desire a Righteous Woman" FCN Vol. 19, Num. 45 (September 12, 2000).

The Repair of the Black Woman

The woman's value equals the existence of every person in the Human family. Why would I say this? It is because without her there is no us, her womb is the laboratory of God himself, and this is where God is manufactured or the continuation of life which is in fact the continuation of that which is the descendant of God himself. Imagine something that valuable being just cast out as garbage, and not protected. Who would not want to protect and invest in the keeping of that which is in essence the most valuable entity, next to God intact and free from corruption and harm's way? Only someone who has a plan for humanity to fall and be that which it was not set up by nature to be.

We see the greatest example of this fall that men have planned for her with the horror of the Trans-Atlantic Slave Trade. This event in the history of the world took a woman who was an example of virtuousness, divine beauty, intelligence, royalty, and literally God representing a feminine expression, and reduced her to the beast of the field, and a whore for the continuation of manufacturing slaves, not a strong people who represent an ancient and divine existence. This process was optimized as we the people found on the continent of Africa, first arrived here in America 459 years ago. The following account is a bearing of witness of the condition that the woman who archaeologists and scientist alike absolutely agree is the mother of all human beings, the first woman, the Black Woman, as she was brought from being a divine woman covered as the mother of Jesus the Christ was, to then being disrobed and made into a whore for her master in slavery.

"Louisa Picquet had even less of a choice. Interviewed after she was "set free", she recalled: "Mr. Williams told me what he bought me for soon as we started for New Orleans. He said if I behave myself he'd treat me well; but, if not, he'd whip me almost to death. He was over forty; I guess pretty near fifty.

Q. Had you any children while in New Orleans?
A. Yes; I had four
Q. Who was their father?
A. Mr. Williams.
Q. Was it known that he was living with you?
A. Everybody knew I was housekeeper, but he never let on that he was the father of my children. I did all the work in his house nobody there but me and the children. When he had company, gentlemen folks, he took them to the hotel.

When Mr. Williams told me what he bought me for I thought, now I shall be committin' adultery, and there's no chance for me, and I'll have to die and be lost. I had this trouble with my soul the whole time. I begin to pray that he might die, so that I might get religion. It was some time before he got sick, He said that if I would promise him that I would go to New York, he would leave me and the children free. In about a month, he died. I didn't cry or nothin', for I was glad he was dead. I was left free, and that made me so glad I could hardly believe it myself" (Dorothy Sterling, ed., We are Your Sisters: Black Women in the Nineteenth Century, p. 24)

What scholars called binary oppression, took place throughout this time period. This further expresses the point of how the Black woman was reduced to a wretched condition to be used as a sexual object for the manufacturing of the Slave Masters' "niggers."

'Binary oppression is defined as the dual oppression that slave women faced because they were black slave women. Slave women experienced binary oppression through the combination of forced productive and reproductive labor. Productive labor consisted of field work, domestic work, and other jobs that both male and female *slaves were forced to perform. Reproductive labor differentiated slave women from men, and was the distinct form of oppression slave women faced. Reproductive labor consisted of forced reproduction and child raising. The children then became property of the owner, allowing the institution of slavery to continue even after the Atlantic Slave Trade ended. Because slave women were seen as property and mere objects, the law did not protect them from instances of rape and abuse. Binary oppression increased the everyday struggles of slave women and created an environment in which they fought against frequent objectification in everyday life.'*

RESISTANCE AND REVOLTS BY ENSLAVED WOMEN
By: Camille LaFleur, J. Kenji Nishikawa, Katie Thomas, Samiyyah Tillman

The sexual intrusion and re-coding of the Black Woman gave way to the Jezebel image and stereotype. Jezebel was bi-product of slavery, and was utilized by the slave master as a justification of why she should be treated no more than a whore; an object of pleasure.

Jezebel

"The Jezebel was a stereotype of the black slave woman that portrayed them as women who wanted, desired, and exuded sex. The Jezebel "was the counter image of the mid-nineteenth-century ideal of the Victorian lady. She did not lead men and children to God; piety was foreign to her. She saw no advantage in prudery, indeed domesticity paled in importance before matters of the flesh"

(WHITE 29) . RESISTANCE AND REVOLTS BY ENSLAVED WOMEN
By: Camille LaFleur, J. Kenji Nishikawa, Katie Thomas, Samiyyah Tillman

"The Jezebel stereotype was a widely used justification by white men and slave owners (even some free and enslaved black men) to rape black women, and use them as sexual objects. Slave women, under certain circumstances, used this stereotype as a tool to their advantage, occasionally manipulating slave owners; however, these acts contributed to the objectification of women as mere sexual objects."

(Camille LaFleur, 2011)

It is evident that the Black Woman was taken from her divinity and goddess culture and way of life she saw when she existed as a Muslim before the travesty of slavery and not just reduced but destroyed. How would she be restored? Who would return her to her divine place as a goddess and align her back to her true nature and way of life; Islam which was so violently ripped from her? Only Allah (God) could.

"Allah (God) came to North America by Himself for you…He came for you, to make you special to Him. And He called you, "Muslim Girl". Girl? Some of the sisters got insulted, "I aint no girl. I'm a woman." Be quiet. To Allah (God), you will always be a girl. To me, you are my sister. But to Allah (God). Who has come to be your Teacher, you are a girl to Him. He wants you in the spirit of a girl, so that He can shape you and mold you."

– The Hon. Min. Louis Farrakhan - Study Guide 19 B; The Key To The Kingdom of God

On July 4th 1930 Allah (God) appeared in the Person of Master W. Fard Muhammad, He brought to the Western Hemisphere the Nation of Islam of which he organized two training units, one for the men, He named the F.O.I., Fruit of Islam, and the other for the women named the M.G.T. and G.C.C., (Muslim Girls' Training and General Civilization Class). Both were set up by Him to train and repair us back to our rightful place as Gods, returning us to our true nature as Muslims, which means one who submits their will to do the will of Allah (God). This nature was destroyed in us as we were brought to America as slaves. He departed in 1934 leaving The Most Hon. Elijah Muhammad as His Messenger with the charge of redeeming the once slave back to his rightful position in the universe. Muhammad worked tirelessly for 40 years giving redemption to the Black man and woman, with a major emphasis on the woman. He teaches that No Nation Can Rise Higher Than It's Woman, and that she is the only heaven for a man. He knew that if we would be brought back to our high standard of civilization, and away from the savage state we now wallow in, he would have to place a major emphasis on the woman. Muhammad left this mission in the capable hands of his extension, and best example The Hon. Min. Louis Farrakhan.

Look at the current condition of Black women; we still see her reflecting the Jezebel that was made by our former slave master.

So now it seems with some of us that it is alright for the Black Woman to make sex tapes to seek "advancement" in this world. The old Jezebel and whore model has become an everyday existence for us. So it's okay that her children eventually sees her on film and thinks that it is necessary to sell themselves to move ahead in this world. I have heard some of us say, 'she making her money' or 'it's keeping her relevant' as a justification on why she should be a prostitute on film.

Do you think the Black Woman, and her image should be reformed, which brings about a woman who is respectful, and ultimately a God? If you say NO then you are a continuation of the ideas of the slave master, so imagine your mother, daughters, sisters and nieces being these women who have prostituted themselves.

Men, do you wish to see women who have become divinely beautiful and refined, who respect themselves and treat you like the gods you are? Look no further, she has arrived in the M.G.T.

"When we speak of repair or reparations, it will take much to repair the damage that our former slave masters and their children have done to the Black man and woman of America and the world. No wonder the Apostle Paul said, "Be ye not conformed to this world, but, be ye transformed by the renewing of your mind." We cannot renew the mind of the male and female until we uproot the idea that now rules our minds and replace it with the ideas of Allah (God). The scholars and scientists of this world do not have a clue as to how to bring about the transformation of human life, particularly the life of the Black man and woman. This is why we Praise Allah (God) for His presence in Master W. Fard Muhammad, and the great work of reform, resurrection and transformation that He began that we are attempting to continue and bring to a new and higher level today. To the men who read this article, cherish a virtuous woman. To the men of the Nation of Islam, seek a female from the class that is producing such women and be good men and husbands to them."

- The Hon. Min. Louis Farrakhan

Reflections of Haziqah

The Courtship process that exists in the Nation of Islam can reform the devalued Black woman that is currently being ravaged from relationships that leave her drained and hurt. The process is an example for the whole world. This process uplifts family where the majority of the current relationships of this world set up an environment where family is destroyed. This is why the courtship process is so valuable in the implementation of relationships, and overall marriage between man and woman, it was the first step on my beautiful journey of being married to an M.G.T.

One might say, "I don't want to get married, I kick it with a few people but I ain't trying to marry them." It is this attitude that is a direct result of our destruction rendered by the horror called slavery. This horror made us as men good breeders, which allowed us to have sexual pleasure with as many women as the slave master allowed us to. This sex without responsibility resulted in the manufacturing of many a slave for the master's work force. The Black Man became the stud and the Black woman continued the activity of Jezebel to the delight of her master.

What has this "just kicking it," or sex without responsibility activity developed in our communities? Has it been productive? Surely that which is harmless would not bring about harm to those involved, as we can tell the purpose of a thing by the results it brings about.

Well the results that are massively present in our communities are single parent households, a great percentage of STD's, and a great deal of woman left emotionally scarred and devalued.
In the Black community, **72** percent of the children are raised in a single parent household. Studies show poverty, a low quality of parenting, and a greater deal of stress negatively affect a large percentage of those children. Children in single parent homes are also more likely to engage in drugs, become incarcerated, and become fluent in self-destructive behaviors early in life.

It is a fact that STD's are running rampant in our community, with the most detrimental of these being HIV/AIDS.
Approximately 13% of America's population is Black, yet we made up (49%) of all new HIV infections in America in 2013
Statistics show that Black men were 70% of the new HIV infection cases within the demographic of all adult and adolescent Blacks, which is seven times higher than White men, twice as high for Latino men, and nearly three times as high for Black women.

Black women make up 66% of new HIV cases among women. HIV/AIDS related illness is currently the leading cause of death for Black women ages **25-34.**

So not only can our behaviors seeking sexual pleasure , without responsibility gravely hinder our children, and our health, many of our women have been left damaged after such relationships. Let's be honest with ourselves every man wants a good woman, and every one woman wants a good man. The epitome of this yearning for the good man and woman is marriage, which many shun because we have not been taught our true selves and how to marry. To bring this about there is a process.

The Courtship process is a solution to the negatives we have spoken of.

What is courting? Merriam Webster defines it as the activities that occur when people are developing a relationship that could lead to marriage or the period of time when such activities occur. So the main intent and motive in this process is to seek information which will let one know if compatibility is present for marriage. In doing so the Most Hon. Elijah Muhammad has taught us our true nature, and culture which was prevalent in us before we were made into the product of slaves. With that in mind, in the process of courtship we do not engage in sex before we have finished our findings of whether or not we are suitable partners, which would then result in marriage, and of course the expression of sexual pleasure with one another.

Some would say that sexual activity is necessary for man and woman to get to know each other. How many of us have known the woman or man we had a child with, or anything else that the horrendous statistics detailed earlier bear witness of? It is a part of our history that we do not have sex before we are married. Our divine history as a people is inclusive of courting to seek a wife, and women living in accords with their divinity remained untouched until marriage. Women would be considered unworthy to be a suitable mate if she had engaged in sex with anyone before her husband.

Well to most of us that sounds old fashioned and unreasonable in today's society where "dating" is present. The linage of the word dating as it relates to men and women derived from the European activity which was to date a prostitute, or have an encounter with her.

Henceforth the Most Hon. Elijah Muhammad's teaching from God Himself which is being given to the Black man and woman by the Hon. Min. Louis Farrakhan in this process of courtship gives way to our history and original culture as gods. It makes us sober minded in the choosing of a mate. Sex stimulates the human being, enhancing the pleasure centers of the brain, like what drugs unnaturally bring about. It is impossible to make a clear decision about a mate if this stimulation takes place, then further down the road you will become sober and wonder "what did I do, who is this person." Just like one would experience after a hangover (smile).

I bear witness to the mathematics of this. Right is going to equal right, as wrong will equal wrong. I did not do the process as we are trained to do and it equaled wrong for me before. Even though my courtships resulted in marriage it turned out wrong, because the courtship process was not adhered to. I was not sober minded in making a decision before. So wrong equaled wrong, resulting in the breakup of families which affected unlikely casualties...the beautiful children. Seeing the effect on the children and myself, I knew I had to submit and do it how the Most Hon. Elijah Muhammad taught us to.

From the first time I saw Haziqah, she represented the valor and dignity of the M.G.T., and I knew that I wanted court her and that I wanted to do it right, so the consequences of doing it wrong would not overtake us.

We began to court, and found out that we enjoyed each other's conversation, which was built on the foundation of the teachings of God to the Most Hon. Elijah Muhammad, our love for the work that The Hon. Min. Louis Farrakhan had taught us of, which was the raising of Black and oppressed people from their wretched condition. We began to learn of each other; past, present and what was desired in the future. All the while we were assessing if we were compatible.

When we would see each other in person it would be in the company of family, so it was not just her I was getting to know but her children, which would become my own by way of marriage. All of us would walk by the lake. She and I side by side so we could talk, and the family close at hand.

To give a visual, it reminded me of one of my favorite films, The Godfather. Michael Corleone knew he needed a suitable mate so that he would come into the full power of the man he needed to be. That power was grounded in a good family structure. So he courted Apollonia, held her to the highest standard because she carried herself with that respect. He spent time with her and got to know her, only with family present so that the nature of man and woman, which is to be attracted to one another did not go within the realm of expressing that attraction because it would not have giving him the clearest understanding of who she was, or vice versa. The family guaranteed that did not happen because their daughter, sister, etc. would have given him pleasure and he was not her husband, which would have made her activities that of a whore...So it is with this beautiful process from Mr. Muhammad. Imagine if Michael would not have married her. Apollonia would have not had sex with him, as she did not do until they were married, and she would still be waiting to give herself to the man that committed to her in marriage, instead of how this world promotes that it should be done where a woman gives herself to any man that just dated her, and over and over again she is left with no man, taking on the activity of a whore, and the Jezebel that the slave master made her into.

So it is with the women of the M.G.T. in this model for relationships called the courtship. They are not deflowered by any man they court, they are reserved for the one that they marry, and this remakes the Black woman into a symbol of beauty and the substance therein.

Love soon developed in Haziqah for me and I for her as we adhered to this beautiful process. The love was so strong since we knew the person, and not through the activity of sex. We had a sober mind, which caused the love to grow more, because we loved Allah's way as the root of our love. I married an M.G.T.

"The greatest gift to any man is a virtuous woman. A man who has such a woman by his side is the most blessed of men, for her virtue is a covering for him and her virtue ensures his future. Our future is made for us by the female. Since sin destroys our future, virtue and righteousness protects and ensures our future, so, wise men in every age have cherished the virtuous woman, and have fought, bled and even died to protect her honor."

The Honorable Minister Farrakhan originally appeared in Volume 19, Number 45 of the Final Call newspaper (September 12, 2000).]

Reflections of Tonja

I know I had to be just as nervous sitting in front of Sdnt. Min. Christopher Muhammad while we were being pre-counseled as I was during our first time meeting in Chicago, Illinois during Saviours' Day 2013 when we had dinner with Tonja's daughter and family. We had a great time and I took a picture of her that would become one of my favorites.

During courtship we did have some high intensity conversations as we began to challenge one another in how we previously looked at life. Our coming together could not contain any of the disempowered data from our past and although we sometimes attempted to hold on to who we believed we had to be at those moments in our past, it would not work in the future we were seeking to create. Did we think of calling it off once or twice? Yes! Did we do it? No! During any of those moments of conflict of getting to know and learn each other at least one of us had the love and discipline to come to the other and seek a way of peace and understanding. For me that came with an apology for my not being as loving as I could be and for her not being as respectful as she could be.

My courtship requirement was that we both read and discuss two books: One was The 5 Love Languages by Gary D. Chapman and the second was by Sarah and Emerson Eggerichs titled: Love & Respect: The Love She Most Desires; The Respect He

Desperately Needs that is based on a biblical principle found in the 5th Chapter of Ephesians. This simple yet effective principle gave us the pause we needed to always look to see where we each could have made an adjustment and brought about better understanding and unity. And the Love Languages helped us better know what we wanted personally so that we could effectively communicate that. Tonja made it clear that it was an absolute must that we go over an in depth viewing of How to Give Birth to a God, Keys toward a Successful Marriage and Love and Duty by The Honorable Minister Louis Farrakhan. Now we were definitely on the right track. After viewing and going over notes taken and points that stood out we knew we were on to something great.

We affectionately called the date we decided we would get married – DDUP (Till Death Do Us Part) and we were married on her 40th birthday, August 15, 2013 at Tilden Botanical Garden surrounded by friends and family and it would be the first time I would be allowed to kiss her and hold her hand.

Courtship does not mean marriage, courtship is a fact finding expedition, so that you might glean the necessary information about the other person as to make an informed and rational decision as to the highest possibility of success and longevity in marriage. Courtship is not to be taken lightly just as with any other court case...it's about the facts and only the facts.

The M.G.T. and the Units of Love:

Tonja On Her Post

Lost Found Muslim - Lesson Number 1

Question 14: What is the meaning of M.G.T. and G.C.C.?

Ans. Muslim Girls' Training and General Civilization Class. This was the name given to the training of women and girls in North America; how to keep house, how to rear their children, how to take care of their husbands, sew, cook and, in general, how to act at home and abroad. These training units were named by our prophet and leader of Islam, W.D. Fard.

Keeping House – Stay in your lane! The home is the M.G.T.'s base of operation and dare I say it's like her corner office on the top floor of the tallest building. And she rules the environment with tact and skill. My wife like myself enjoys a little bit of organized clutter when it came to the office and study spaces, but heaven help you if you leave something in a place it didn't belong any place else. She was meticulous when it came to the bedroom and the kitchen. She would make it a point to ensure that all floors were mopped, dishes done, beds made and bathrooms completely cleaned prior to my arrival home from a week of speaking. And all of this was done while she still attended Friday Night Study Group and cooked dinner. However keeping of house was not limited to the structure we called home, but most importantly the 'House of Allah (God)' was kept clean...our minds! Tonja was committed to making sure that we all were cleaning up our mental lives as well. The external reality being a reflection of our internal reality we strove daily to be clean both 'internally and externally'.

How To Cook - "You gotta try this...!" Growing up I was never really big on food, however being married to Tonja changed all that. At the beginning of our journey together she would ask me: "What would you like me to fix you for dinner?" or "what do you have a taste for?" Now my standard reply was always "it doesn't matter, whatever you cook is fine, I'm good with Bean Soup every day." While she heard my words every time, deep down inside I think my answers conflicted with her religion. Tonja would always seek out the most elaborate meals she could whether it came from 'The Muslim Cookbook' or from something she found online from Martha Stewart. She would always take her time and start early enough in the day so as to not have to rush the meal and insure it was done with love. So sure we would have Bean Soup, with a side of love.

In her effort to streamline our food production (yes she ran it like a serious business – the business of a healthy family) she decided to develop a monthly menu plan. This menu plan would allow her to purchase all of the main staple foods at one time and weekly shop for the fresh foods needed to prepare the meals for the week. Now I don't know about her but I absolutely loved this idea because it took me back to the excitement I felt in elementary school when you looked on the cafeteria lunch schedule and you knew that week they were going to be serving pittsburgers (look it up online) and the next day pizza. Knowing what was going to be coming up took the guess work out of meal preparation and removed all the stress from daily having to run to the store and find something wholesome to eat. I should have known that when she got her M.G.T. study books on How to Eat to Live and How To Cook it was going to be some serious changes around our home. Being vegetarian always provides excitement in but Tonja knew that when The Honorable Minister Louis Farrakhan requested that we eliminate meat from our diet back in 1994 he said it to save our lives so it was food love at first sight because we both shared the same food desires that were in line with the teachings of Master Fard Muhammad in How To Eat To Live books 1 and 2.

Spiritual food are like multi-vitamins for the soul and we made sure we took our daily multi. We would often say "I think we have more books than we have house..." Being avid readers and lovers of study we never passed up an opportunity to purchase a book recommended by someone or even something we seen in a movie that looked like it might be of some value in our lives. With subjects ranging from Religion to Chemistry, Mechanical to Relationships we made it a point to be well rounded in our studies. We understood as students of The Most Honorable Elijah Muhammad and his best student The Honorable Louis Farrakhan that it was the Mental Food that gave us the mind to know what physical foods to eat and since the saying goes: "you are what you eat." We kept those Wednesday and Friday night study sessions in high demand in our schedule of activities. While my travel takes me away from home 3 weeks per month, Tonja tried to make every study session humanly possible and would feel bad if she missed one.

Rearing Children - It took a lot for her to give birth to her only child from her previous relationship and that child came to birth after several 'failed' attempts and to only have that child be born at a very low birth weight with doctors not knowing if she would survive. With much tragedy and struggle Tonja was committed to being the best mother around. Never wanting her daughter out of her sight and always being the best example, she made it a point to show her what a Muslim Woman in the Nation of Islam looks and acts like.

Muhammad University of Islam (M.U.I.) in San Francisco was her original base of operations and as a committed believer and mother she taught classes at the school often not being compensated because she believed in having independent education and was willing to sacrifice some economics to see our children free and educated by our own. Ever the watchful eye she maintained influence over the life that Allah blessed to come through her.

Moving to Phoenix was exciting and she decided years before she ever gave birth that she would never commit her children to the public school system. Home schooling allowed her to be an even more active mother and guide and as she put it: "The home environment provides the extra layer of security" to keep her daughter on task. Tonja sought to maintain influence even over the digital goings on of the child never leaving her daughter to her own devices and the lure of Satan's contrary world to capture our children.

Although Tonja made it clear to me that we would not be getting married if I did not desire more children. She wanted more, more and still more and I applauded her for that desire as she told me that her love for me gave her an even stronger desire to want to reproduce the love that we brought into each other's lives. So even though she wanted children from our new union, Allah being the best knower and best of planners she was allowed to be a big sister and aunt to many young brothers and sisters over the 20 years she was a registered member of The Nation of Islam. Children to have to "come from you" when they by the grace of Allah see the love you have for them thus causing them to want to "come to you".

How To Act At Home – Even Tempered! If consistency and constancy had to be given a singular human name it would be Tonja. My being a very spirited and high energy person provided the excitement of the moment and Tonja provided the icing on the energy cake. Always eager to engage me in dialog, yet definitely keeping her discipline and high civilization right out front. Oh yes make no mistake, she could get edgy (she is in The Nation you know) and I would say to her at those more edgier times..."Babe less East Oakland and more Oakland Hills please!" She carried herself as a woman of God knowing that the home we would build would be her base and not her place.

Some people play games because they are of this current world's life but the games Tonja made up for our family were designed to bring us all closer together. Playing games like "Name that lecture", "Is it in the book?" and also games that brought us closer as a couple that would allow us to open up even deeper to one another about dreams, hopes and aspirations for our future. She would often make up her own game cards and rules (that I had to abide by) and she was serious about her creation.

How to act at home is really an exercise in how to be pleasant and amenable and she taught us well. You see in order to have a peaceful home the people of the home must be a people of peace and home is the place you get the chance to practice being the person you desire to be.

Sewing – Always frugal, not always out of necessity but as a principle of the training she was given in M.G.T. Class. Tonja wasn't an expert seamstress, but the skills she gained through her class gave her the confidence and ability to do what many women and girls have long forgotten.

Once we had our wedding date set (we affectionately referred to it as D.D.U.P. – till Death Do Us Part) Tonja went to work on designing a dress she could be proud of and one I would adore. She hunted for days for just the right fabric and once found she cut the pattern to precision. She worked on this dress daily and even called me crying one day saying she accidentally had sewn through her finger while working on the dress late into the night while sleepy. She constructed the head covering and sash and meticulously made sure it all flowed together. She was so committed to working this unit of training out, she even made a dress for her daughter to wear.

Both dresses were magnificent creations and on August 15, 2013 she wore that dress with pride.

Oh I almost forgot to tell you, we even had a matching bow tie cut from the same fabric as her dress made...unity even at the smallest level is needed. However I must say to you that physical sewing is only one aspect of that training unit.

Tonja had an ability to sew broken hearts, lives and relationships together by using the needle of truth and the thread of love. Never one to allow the holding of grudges, she constantly exhorted all she knew to find a way to atone and repair their relationships with others.

So whether the situation required a simple stitch, a little hemming work or you had to break out the Serger...creating a quilt of love and unity was important to her...how about you?

How to act abroad – Always helping (a helper's helper).

"Final Call or Bean Pie my Brother?" When we first met and after the first month when she finally allowed me to speak to her on the phone I told her I would call her on a Thursday afternoon just to check in with her and she told me she would be busy. Asking what she had in the works she said: "Sister Kim and I go out with the Final Call and our Bean Pies because we have a store owner a few doors down from the Mosque that allows us offer them in front of the store to customers coming in and out." My first thought: "Wow!"

How To Take Care of Husbands

– When it came to me Tonja had her work cut out for her. With the skill of a master chef she was able to put the right ingredients (temperament, love, encouragement, correction, forgiveness etc.) together to get the best out of me.

Care is defined as: 1. to watch over; be responsible for. 2. to act on; deal with; attend to: To know how best to care for a person you first must know the function or purpose of said person. You must know of their current and potential abilities and once known, it is wise to study the person deeply in an effort to better understand where they are in that moment in time that you might properly guide them toward their full self.

Tonja studied me like the student she was. I always admired how she could remember even the smallest details of most lectures and writings as it related to The Teachings. She approached her life as a student always willing to learn and as my wife she took to her studies with laser like precision.

She asked questions of me that I thought were excessive but in trying to best understand a person very necessary. She watched my movements and studied my patterns. Tonja knew that if she was to assist in making a Man for God that she had to understand the material she was working with in order to best apply the right prescription. Where I was impatient she demonstrated patience. Where I was unforgiving she forgave me and showed me reasons to forgive. Where I was arrogant she showed me the benefits of being humble and where I was unwilling to serve others she took the lead and not only served others but served me as well.

She took care of our home and the matters of our home while I was away speaking. Tonja handled the responsibilities and business of the bakery we co-owned, picking up supplies, delivering to customers, collecting money and getting new clients. She took pride in supporting every endeavor I brought to her. Anything new at the Mosque we got involved in she supported and backed with her advice and efforts.

Now I have to say that I always loved her surprises. From 'Rodney's Sugar Lip Scrub', 'Rodney's Working Man Foot Soak', Homemade deodorant and toothpaste all the way to the 'Love tent' she set up in the house using the dining room table and chairs so we could sit and hold hands and eat a fancy dessert she created that day(just to break the monotony). Tonja always found a way to connect with me at a very simple yet deep level by finding new ways to surprise my mind.

Taking care of a husband is no small feat as you must not only know the person you are to take care of but you must also have a deep understanding of what Allah (God) wants out of the person. I have had several people ask me: "Brother what lesson have you gotten out of what has happened?" And my answer is found in Tonja's beginning:

The parents that raised Tonja were not her biological mother and father, they were her aunt and uncle. Her biological mother out of her love for her sister who could not give birth, decided with her husband that they would have another baby and give the baby to the sister and her husband. So in the last month of the pregnancy her biological mother moved to California to have the baby and once the baby was born on August 15, 1973 she gave the baby to her sister and departed back to her home state. Never referring to Tonja as her daughter but her niece, leaving that title to her sister and husband Tonja was reared with love and care by two wonderful parents.

You see Tonja was conceived out of a selfless love that very few will ever know from another person and the lesson that she by Allah's permission came to teach me was how to love at a much deeper level than I ever thought possible. And that level of love can be found in the following verses in the Bible:

1 Corinthians 13:1-10

1 If I speak with the tongues of men and of angels, but have not love, I am become sounding brass, or a clanging cymbal.

2 And if I have the gift of prophecy, and know all mysteries and all knowledge; and if I have all faith, so as to remove mountains, but have not love, I am nothing.

3 And if I bestow all my goods to feed the poor, and if I give my body to be burned, but have not love, it profits me nothing.

4 Love suffers long, and is kind; love envies not; love lifts not itself, is not puffed up,

5 does not behave itself unseemly, seeks not its own, is not provoked, and takes no account of evil;

6 rejoices not in unrighteousness, but rejoices with the truth;

7 bares all things, believes all things, hopes for all things, and endures all things.

8 Love never fails: but whether there be prophecies, they shall be done away; whether there be tongues, they shall cease; whether there be knowledge, it shall be done away.

9 For we know in part, and we prophesy in part;

10 but when that which is perfect is come, that which is in part shall be done away.

RECEIVING HEAVEN at Home

– Haziqah's Comfort

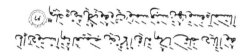

It is He who created for you all of that which is on the earth. Then He directed Himself to the heaven, [His being above all creation], and made them seven heavens, and He is Knowing of all things.

"The Aim of the Honorable Elijah Muhammad is the Reformation of both the Black man and the Black woman, with special attention on the Black woman, because, as He has said, "Where there are no decent women, there are no decent men, for the Black woman is the Mother of Civilization."

The Reformation of the Black man must include a reformation of his view of himself and the Black woman, who is his second self, His reformation must include the removal of any and all tendencies to abuse the Black woman and/ or to use her as an instrument of sexual pleasure without accepting responsibilities imposed upon us by Allah (God) when in our relationships with the female.

It is out of the Desire and Will of Allah (God) for the Reformation of the male and female that He set up two independent classes for their instruction: The Fruit of Islam and the Muslim Girls Training and General Civilization Class."

– The Hon. Min. Louis Farrakhan from Study Guide 18: Rising Above Emotion Into The Thinking of God

I would come home to paradise daily in the arms of a Black woman, an M.G.T. What brother does not want to come home to peace? A man is lying to you straight up if he would say he didn't want that. I recall a time where in discussion with the brothers at the office, I said that I could not wait to get home to my wife and that I was trying to remember what was on the menu for today. They responded "the menu." I said yes sir; my wife prepares a weekly menu and I approved of the menu. They were thoroughly impressed, and were somewhat familiar with how Haziqah would serve with divinity.

When we would have business gatherings at the office she would host, utilizing her supreme training from the M.G.T.- G.C.C., laying out a table so tantalizing to the eye, and the pallet, all while dressed in the dress of an M.G.T. covered from head to toe. She loved to serve, and the people loved her. The people were attracted to the greatness, and reform that God placed in the M.G.T., they looked at her with awe wherever we traveled. The grocery store it did not matter Haziqah attracted the eye of the people and she loved them. My beloved mother in law would tell me how she would be driving down the street and see our brothers sagging and with a loving and firm word she would roll down the window and say pull up your pants Black man, and they would respond, "Yes ma'am," because they know she cared, while carrying herself with respect.

Being involved with the hip-hop community, as well as being a writer, I would have interviews with hip-hop artists, and cover concerts and so forth. If the place was befitting of her, I would take her with me. Yet again she would be would be representing the M.G.T. and its model for the respect of Black women wherever she was. If we were backstage, on a tour bus, or at the radio station, she was there as a shining example. The Most Hon. Elijah Muhammad teaches us to be a clean glass, in a world of dirty glasses, and that the people would surely love to drink from a clean glass. At home and abroad she was that clean glass. Our brothers in the hip-hop community are used to the blatant disrespect of our women; henceforth this is why Muhammad's model of respect of women is so important. I have literally seen our brothers in the settings of rap music industry yield to the M.G.T., my wife Haziqah with the utmost respect.

Heaven in the form of this Black woman was not just the homemade wheat bread, food holistically prepared, the care for our children that we had as a blended family, her making me clothes, or our beautiful expressions of love, it was sometimes just simply her asking me, "Hassan let me help, what I can do?" Then she would be found helping to bring comfort to me knowing that my love for her was being backed by my duty to her and the family. Every man wants a woman that he can call his heaven, I am thankful that the M.G.T. instructors are preparing them.

OVERCOMMING the Loss of Haziqah

From the moment my pregnant wife, Haziqah Safiyah Muhammad, was admitted into the hospital from a blood clot in her brain, I asked Allah (God) to intervene and heal her. We were blessed to galvanize prayer warriors, and people of good will to focus on her recovery. We in her room in the ICU called it "the undying faith walk". The daily ups and down were straining to the family, yet we kept our faith that she would make a full recovery no matter what the doctors were saying. She was unconscious for most of the time she was in the hospital, yet we even got a chance to see the baby via ultrasound, which was 10 weeks old, and the doctors said had a strong heartbeat. The neurologists thought they were witnessing a miracle at times when she became responsive, and opened her eyes and looked around the room when Bro. Student Min. Jeffery Muhammad, who is the Dallas Representative of The Hon. Min. Louis Farrakhan and the Nation of Islam said "Sister Haziqah the Hon. Min. Louis Farrakhan wants you at the meeting tonight" as he was scheduled to speak to the Believers. We were all so thankful. She would even squeeze my hand and looked into my eyes, as she did her mother, and responded to her sister, cousin, and her sister's in the M.G.T. as well. Our daughter Nailah sung to her and she responded and opened her eyes to her also. With all this happening, in the midst of this severe illness, we were hopeful.

Our hope of her returning was ended on March 10ᵗʰ, 2014 when she was pronounced brain dead and then she passed. I cannot explain my feeling; she was my best friend next to God himself. I could not believe it. I had not come to grips with it; I wanted her to just wake up so we could do what we use to do. I would miss praying with her, talking with her, holding her, kissing her, us texting back and forth throughout the day, going and surprising her with a visit to Muhammad University of Islam which she worked for, I would miss expressing our love for each other which we did whenever we were together.

It became real when I went to get the children and bring them to the hospital and told them that their mother had passed. They had lost their mother; they would never be able to have her present in the physical form. They would never be able to discuss growing up and gain her advice, and receive so many attributes that a child receives from its mother, she was gone.

Our family received so much overwhelming love from our Nation represented by Muhammad Mosque No. 48 in Dallas, TX, and the Southwest Region. Everyone from the mosque was there for the 8 days she was in the ICU. Brothers and Sisters from Kansas City, MO which is where my wife was from, and all over our Nation helped tremendously. The beautiful people of Evergreen Funeral home which allowed us to bury her the way all of our ancient people have been buried, utilizing the Islamic culture.

The children were uplifted when I told them that the son of the Most Hon. Elijah Muhammad, Ishmael Muhammad, who is the National Assistant to the Hon. Min. Louis Farrakhan, had called with his concern for them and his expression of the UNDYING duty their mother exhibited for our Nation in its service for our people and all oppressed.

They maintained further high spirits when I told them that Sister Sandy, our National M.G.T.-G.C.C. Student Captain had called. Sister Sandy was so very concerned and sincere. She being charged with the awesome responsibility of being over the training of every woman in the Nation of Islam; which takes place in the M.G.T. / G.C.C., told me such inspiring words about my wife. She said, "Your wife was one of my best helpers" as she continued to talk of the love she had for Haziqah. The children were so happy to hear this, it gave them a sense of pride in regards to their mother. It made the mission she gave her life daily for take on a new appreciation in them, with this aspect in mind she lived, because her work was UNDYING.

Although I was so inspired, I was also saddened, and I thought why Allah would allow a great helper of His to pass. I knew since He allowed it, it had to be for a great purpose. It was all a part of His mathematical equation. Those words from Brother Ishmael and Sister Sandy, gave way for me to express to the children how she would live through them and us if we keep her legacy alive with our actions. Even through our pain I ask them: "What would Haziqah do?" Would your mother approve of this, or that as a standard of one who follows the standards of God Himself, and His Christ?

I am still attempting to process the loss of my best friend and wife, a gift from Allah (God) Himself. The best thing we can do to honor her life, is to find our purpose so that we would be found working to better our neighborhoods, community, and world. My wife was always found working with this cause in mind. She gave her life daily to see Black Women lifted from the bowels of disrespect to the standard of goddesses...which she showed and proved as a member of the M.G.T.-G.C.C. that she loved so intensely.

The best way to deal with her passing is to keep her legacy alive, continuing to do the work she committed her life to... and that is the rise of the Black Man and Woman, and all oppressed peoples. My focus for the last 8 years has particularly been our youth that are dying in the streets. My wife helped us as Dynasty Hip-Hop Mentoring Program got youth off the streets using hip-hop.

So I got back to work, working through my pain, not wallowing, so I would not become depressed. We must work, even as we mourn. There is not a moment I don't think about the wife I was blessed with, she was a gift from Him, and to Him she returned. Yet the work of raising our people is a work my wife and I committed our lives to. Dynasty Hip-Hop Mentoring Program would begin to work more and more in the streets and in schools. Bro James and I doing what we loved best became therapeutic to me. And even though I am still pained by the loss, I feel better seeing our youths lives being saved from the traps set up for them in the streets which aims to kill them all.

This loss allowed me to be here for my beloved brother Rodney whom since the passing of our wives we have checked on each other daily. Which is a great help because you really don't know what to expect with this painful event until you have experienced it, so it was in Allah's plan that I experienced it to be there for him, and he there for me.

As you reflect on our trial, let the energy not be in vain to settle whatever difference we have with our spouse, or any other family member. We do this best by putting into action the atonement process.

During Minister Farrakhan's address at The Million Man March, he outlined Eight Principle Steps in the Atonement Process. Simply stated, they are as follows:

1. Point out the wrong.

2. Acknowledge the wrong.

3. Confess the Fault.

4. Repent.

5. Atone.

6. Forgive.

7. Reconcile and Restore.

8. Perfect Union with God.

"When these Eight Principle Steps are put into practice, it will bring about a Healing on our Planet and open up the Way to a Culture of World Peace based on genuine love and Forgiveness."
- Mother Tynnetta Muhammad - The Final Call Web Post 04-23-2002

I am asking Allah (God) to intervene and open your heart for what I am about to say this day, I petition you with all of my being to LOVE TODAY, please, please, please, don't wait until tomorrow, it might be too late. Put yourself in my shoes for just a moment. As there is not a moment that goes by that I don't think of my wife's passing. I miss praying with her, talking with her, holding her, kissing her, us texting back and forth throughout the day, going and surprising her with a visit to our school which she worked for, I miss expressing our love for each other which we did whenever we were together.

Imagine those things you would miss about your love one if they were gone forever, and then go do them TODAY. If you have strife and issues with them tell them TODAY, "TODAY IS A NEW DAY, I LOVE YOU AND WANT TO TELL YOU NOW, THANKFUL THAT WE STILL CAN, AS I THOUGHT ABOUT WHAT IT WOULD BE LIKE IF WE WERE GONE FROM EACH OTHER FOREVER." I guarantee you will see a change and then go forth and work the love. Put the steps of atonement in action. Be thankful for the blessing to do all that you would miss, because everyone can't. WE CANT SAY I LOVE YOU, AND I WILL SEE YOU WHEN I GET HOME AND LOOK AT OUR WIVES FACES, AND SEE THEM LIGHT UP WITH LOVE,

The choice is yours, LOVE NOW, or LIVE WITH REGRET later.

OVERCOMMING the Loss of Tonja

The day the earth stood still! It was April 8, 2014, 468 days after we met, 236 days after our wedding day at Tilden Botanical Gardens, 10 days after our hike up Superstition Mountain, 2 days after she fell ill from something she ate, and 1 day after I was to ever see her alive again.

The call came in at about 3:11PM and the earth stood still and time seemed to have stopped that my wife, companion and friend, "didn't make it". "But how, no, oh Allah!" I was in the process of rushing back to Phoenix on the next available flight to get to her side.

Let me take you to the beginning. Friday April 4th I arrived home from travel and Tonja picked me up from the airport as usual. Gave me her best As-Salaam Alaikum as I entered the car and a kiss on the cheek. The drive home was smooth and she asked me as she normally would: "Are you hungry because I made you something?" "Yes ma'am I haven't eaten at all today." After arriving home we part ways, her into the kitchen and me to go get the "travel dust" off me with a shower. Exiting the shower I put on the P.J.'s and fresh shirt she has perfectly laid out for me. As I am putting on socks she enters the room with self-made "Rodney's Foot Balm" and tells me to "take those socks off." After taking good care of my aching feet we dine on fresh lentil soup, homemade bread and salad. Dinner done we retreat to watch our show. Yes! We made an agreement during courtship that we would wait until I got home and watch Scandal together so we could science up what the show was selling to our people that week...Saturday morning was the usual. Me off to deliver pies and she off to M.G.T. Class. Sunday is where the story takes its turn.

Tonja decided she didn't want to overdo it that day and decided to stay home from the meeting as she was scheduled to accompany a few other sisters to a Native American POW WOW in Fort McDowell, Arizona.

I attended a fellowship meeting with our local student minister to a nearby church and arrived back home very close to the time she needed to leave to meet with the sisters. I told her she could leave our 13 year old daughter home so that she could have some adult sister time (this we never did before as I always insisted that her daughter accompany her everyplace). I wanted her to just enjoy the day so "the child stays with me and we can watch some movies and strengthen our bond" and she agreed. As I pulled up to our home she was waiting in the drive way in full garment ready to jump in and go. We kissed, exchanged "I Love You" and I told her to "have a good time". She drove away closer toward our destiny.

The call came in at **5:30PM** that said: "Brother Rodney we are bringing your wife home, she got really sick after something she ate..." "O.K. come on I'm here waiting..." Once my wife and the sisters arrived at my home I carried my wife into our home where she got comfortable and yet still expelling stomach contents. After taking the sisters home I got some supplies from the grocery store to assist in nursing her back to health (more water, drinks to add electrolytes and sparkling waters to calm the stomach). She finally calmed her stomach down by **8:45PM** and was bundled up as I lay next to her thankful that she was now able to rest. I will not bore you with the smallest of details. I was scheduled to fly to California the next morning and not really wanting to leave I made some phone calls to have one of her best sister friends come by the house to help in nursing her back to health. The sister agreed. I sent text messages to some of her remote sister friends letting them know to "ASA call ya sister, she is a little under the weather so call and lift her spirits please." The taxi picked me up at **8:35AM** and I kissed her and told her how much I loved her and that I would call when I got to the airport. This would be the last time we would see one another again and the last time I would be allowed to kiss her lips and tell her that I loved her.

My travel time was smooth and I made my normal phone calls to "check in", Sister Jevedia Muhammad made it to the house and brought massive amounts of supplies including soups, ice cube broths and electrolyte drinks to help and spent hours with her and Madinah. Tonja and I spoke again that night before bed and she told me that her stomach was still hurting but she was feeling a little better but didn't think that she was going to go into a new job she just secured that next day. I agreed that she should rest and go out the next day and "get some sun on your face and just relax love..." We exchanged 'I Love You' and I let her know I would call her in the morning to check on them.

Tuesday morning was starting like every other morning, I made my prayers, got dressed and let my mother whose home I was staying in while in California speaking that I would talk with her later that night. During my drive I call Tonja at 6:30am to check in and she sounded great, and in excellent spirits. I told her it would be good to get out of that bed and get to the couch and let the T.V. watch her and also to get outside and get some sunlight. She agreed that would be a good idea. "Are you drinking your water and trying to eat a little Love?" I asked. She replied that she was and that she hated throwing up...we both laughed as this was something she told me during our courtship (why I had no idea). It might have been under the context of having more children and morning sickness. After getting off the phone I continued my drive and got set up to teach my class for the day.

8:30AM I open the doors to allow the students to check in and get seated and I call home to check in. Madinah answered the phone and I asked "hey baby girl what's going on?" she replied "she threw up again and won't get out the bed like you said". After being asked to put me on speaker phone I chided Tonja to "come on sweetheart don't stay in that bed, try to get moving just a little even if just to the couch and open up the windows to get some fresh air and sunlight." She was complaining that her stomach still hurt. I asked her "do you want to go to the hospital love?" We agreed that she needed to go at this point. I called several local believers including the student minister and Sister Jevedia started on her way to the home to take her to the hospital. I called back home and Madinah told me that she had another accident and threw up again. I told her to hang up and "call 911 now!" She called 911 and I called Sister Jevedia again to update her and find out how close she was to arrival. She was 7 minutes away and I called back home several times unable to get an answer. After finally picking up again Madinah informed me that "I don't think she is breathing!" "Oh Allah no!" was my reply and "do CPR or whatever you know how to do please Madinah, go to the neighbor's house and ask for help please!" she exclaimed that "the paramedics are here!" "O.K. yes ma'am let them do their work." I called Sister Jevedia again to update her and find out how far away she was and she was just pulling up and told me that she would let me know what hospital they were taking Tonja to.

I called my client and informed them of what was happening and that I would be needing a flight as soon as possible back to Phoenix due to my wife being in the hospital. I began teaching my students at 9:00AM and made more phone calls at the first beak at 10:30AM and Sister Jevedia informed me that the doctors said that Tonja is "not doing so well". I will not give you all of the details of the many phone calls that came after. But there is one in particular that I know as a reader you would want to know about. Sister Jevedia called me and said: "Brother Asaad they are trying to stabilize her and had to put a breathing tube in because she was not breathing on her own." "Yes ma'am" was my reply. I asked "is it possible that you can let me talk to Tonja so I can let her know that I am on my way to her now?" she said "yes sir let me make that happen." She was able to get me on speaker so I could talk to Tonja. "Babe I am on my way Love, I know you don't like being alone and I am coming home now so please hold on babe, I love you, sweetheart and I will be there soon, I love you!" I thanked Sister Jevedia and I started my journey to the airport to await my 4:45 flight to Phoenix that would have me arrive at 6:00PM. And while waiting for my flight, praying to Allah that His will be done in our lives and asking Him to heal my wife...

As I stood there waiting I got the call from Sister Jevedia at about 3:11PM and the earth stood still and time seemed to have stopped, that my wife, companion and friend, "didn't make it". "But how, no, oh Allah!" And this is how we begin the next part of this wonderful journey called my life.

Arriving in Phoenix at 6:00PM I was escorted by the F.O.I. to the hospital where I met the local student minister and secretary and we were taken down to the basement of the hospital. After walking for what seemed like a mile I entered a hall way and there was a gurney in the hall with a white sheet covering it. The RN prepped me that there were still breathing tubes and things in place and "do not be alarmed". I thanked him for the heads up and he pulled back the sheet and there she was. The lifeless remains of a woman that was so full of love, so full of hope, so full of the spirit of Allah and service to our people, no longer moving, talking or smiling. I whispered in her ear "Allah-U-Akbar, I love you Love and I am so sorry I wasn't here for you. Thank you so much for loving me." I kissed her cold forehead and I turned and said "O.K. let's go!" The real work begins NOW!

That night at home was the worst night of my life until then and the morning was even worse. That night I cleaned the room from the remnants of emergency staff work and I prayed, prayed, and prayed to Allah. I will tell you the details of these payers when I see you in the classes we will be doing because I want you to look into my heart and see my face when I tell you these things that if written down would lose the power of what Allah has for us all.

That Wednesday afternoon is where the healing began. My prayers were about to be answered with 7 talks / phone calls that I would ultimately receive. The first Angel of Allah came in the person of Brother Eric Ahad Muhammad as he sat in a hospital room recovering from a major car accident (my wife had assisted his family greatly during his time of trial and visited nearly daily including the watching of his and Sister Jevedia's daughter). Brother Eric said this to me from his heart: "Brother Rodney you need to go get quiet and Allah and your wife will speak to you and let you know what you need to do next. And let me ask you this: Do you love your wife more than you love Allah?" I said "no sir!" he said "why?" I replied "because Allah gave her to me" and he said "exactly so she is His servant and He can call back to Himself any of His servants is that right?" "yes sir that is correct", he said "brother go home and Allah will speak to you just pray and get quiet."

I arrived home that Wednesday night and did as requested and after prayer that next morning the first call I got was from the second Angel of Allah in the person of Brother Jihad Hassan Muhammad who lost his wife just 30 short days before and was the topic of conversation between Tonja and myself when he was in the throes of his trial. Brother Jihad offered his ear, his love and his service to me, a brother he had never met once in life and told me part of his journey and gave me words of comfort: "seek refuge in Allah and know that you can call me anytime you need to talk or anything".

The 3rd and next Angel of Allah came in the person of Dr. Abdul Alim Muhammad the Minister of Health and Human Services of the Nation of Islam. He shared with me his experiences losing his wife and shared with me how using the technology of the Dianetic Assist helped him greatly along with prayer.

The 4th and next Angel of Allah came in the person of Bro. Student Minister Abel Muhammad. Who not only offered words of comfort and uplift he demonstrated how deep our brotherhood is. Being original people our open enemy would have everyone believe that there is a disconnect between Black People and Spanish Speaking or Latino Peoples and I can tell you that Brother Abel and others in and outside The Nation of Islam are living proof that we are in fact one people. Brother Abel gave me the jewel of universal brotherhood and he didn't even know how during the courtship with my wife she was in the Bay Area and excited to see him at an event and called me and asked if it would be improper is she asked him if she could take a picture with him and of him.

Now the 5th Angel of Allah came in the person of Student Minster Ishmael Muhammad the student national assistant to The Honorable Minister Louis Farrakhan. This call came as a total surprise to me as I have met him over the years and admired him from afar but to actually speak with him was a highlight of this journey. He shared with me key verses from the Holy Qur'an and offered his assistance in any way needed and his sincerity came thought the phone loud and clear.

The 6th Angel of Allah came in the person of Student Minister of the Western Region Tony Muhammad. Now this was a power packed call. If you know anything about Brother Tony he is on fire with the spirit of Allah with his love for our people and the believers. His spirit of joy and hope inspired me even more...and before we concluded the call he said to me these words: "Man Brother Rodney...I called you to lift your spirit and you done fired me all up!" I love having brothers like Brother Tony in my life, fired up and ready to go to work to save our people (even if they are already in the house).

The 7th and final Angel of Allah came in the person of Student National M.G.T. Captain Sandy Muhammad. When I got the call from her office my smile had to have been a mile wide. I knew how completely Tonja loved her class and the study they are on. And to receive that call let me know how serious the sisterhood of The Nation of Islam is. I informed the sister that called how my wife "loved her class" and "out of all the calls I have gotten this one was most important to me" as it related to Tonja being in the M.G.T. and G.C.C. Sister Sandy was even kind enough to have delivered a Peace Lily plant that has been brightening up our home since it arrived and serves as a reminder of the love of the sisterhood.

Now I received another call and this one wasn't from an Angel of Allah but came from Allah's Servant in Our midst The Honorable Minister Louis Farrakhan. His secretary made calls per his request for "clear pictures of my wife's face so that he could see her". I was elated and puzzled and got those pictures sent off in record time I tell you. I hope to one day ask my Minister what his reason was because I know his request is deeper than anything I could ever imagine.

While in the whirlwind of this test and trial I decided to share my experience with those who loved and had been directly impacted by my wife. I thought it would be selfish of me and not in accord with her legacy if I attempted to make her transition "all about me". So I took to social media to share my faith in Allah, tears, desires and deepened purpose with all who would listen. I am thankful to my Brother Philip A. Muhammad of the L.O.T.C.

(Lions Out The Cage) who took the action of putting together a memorial page in honor of my wife who told me "I don't want you hanging around with that Philip, because every time you talk with him you get all fired up talking about Lions Out The Cage over here!" (smile) She loved our demonstration of brotherhood and that was her joking way of saying keep the brotherhood tight. That website allowed those who wanted to assist in laying our sister to final rest as a Muslim, to donate much needed funds to secure our sister. I am eternally thankful to Imam Ahmad Shqeirat of the Islamic Center of Tempe, AZ who opened up the Center to us so that the M.G.T. could properly prepare the body of our sister and allowing us to perform the Salat al-Janazah and to all who gave to see our sister given a proper Salat al-Janazah and burial in accord with the teachings of Islam and the monies above the cost have been donated to the Saviours' Day Gift 2015 in the name of Sister Tonja Muhammad and you can continue to support the Saviours' Day Gift Drive by going to www.ILoveFarrakhan.com and by Allah's permission I intend on completing her Saviours' Day Gift with your help. I am also thankful to all those that drove, flew and sent cards of uplift and love, words cannot adequately express my gratitude so instead of trying to write those words I want to do a mighty work to show my gratitude. This trial has opened me up to what I believe is my purpose and the very thing that Tonja was encouraging me to do just one week prior and that is to do more to help the believing body using my gifts and talents as a speaker and mentor.

So I constantly pray to Allah (God) that He will continue to use myself and Brother Jihad to help strengthen marriages and relationships.

As I said in my prayers to Allah the night Tonja transitioned: "Here I am Allah, choose me!" You see the day the earth stood still was really the day I found my faith in Allah.

Love TODAY - Gratitude

Be quick to forgive and perception in the abberated mind is not reality. Yes all couples striving to be married will have their share of what we call "high level discussions" but at the end of it all we must be sure that the words of Allah (God) and The Teachings we have been given are the measure by which we judge the validity of our points. Never to go to bed angry even if still filled with concern about the discussion. Say this often "I wouldn't waste any life moments on that", when something comes up that would be a distraction from your path toward being married (unification of a man and woman wrapped in the bosom of Allah).

The day Sister Tonja made her transition I told her I loved her like I had nearly every one of those 236 days we were together and I meant it every time. So no matter the weather, the time or the circumstance please demonstrate LOVE (duty)!

If you had advance knowledge that your spouse was going to die in two days what would you be doing on Day 1? Would the time be spent in conflict, disappointment and strife? Would that small thing that you might have thought at the time was a big thing be so utterly important? Would you spend the early part of Day 2 researching online or down at the local courthouse how to file divorce papers? How would you talk? What would you say? I ask that for 19 minutes of this day (after you finish reading this book), you step into my shoes and imagine a day the earth stands still and you get a call that says: "your spouse didn't make it" and later that night you walk down a hospital basement hallway. And as the Nurse pulls back the white sheet and you see the lifeless body of what was once your warm and loving spouse and you kiss their cold forehead and say to them..."I'm sorry!"

The Holy Qur'an informs us that Allah hates divorce and He hates ingratitude and we should also.

Author Biography's

Jihad Hassan Muhammad, was born in St. Louis, MO, where he, influenced by hip-hop, would at the early age of 16, become a follower of The Most Hon. Elijah Muhammad, under the leadership of The Hon. Min. Louis Farrakhan, and a registered member of the Nation of Islam.

The co-founder of Dynasty Hip-Hop Inc. Mentoring Program, an organization that utilizes hip-hop and its culture to get at-risk youth off the streets, and out of violent activity. Dynasty has enlisted the help of many industry professionals like 35 time platinum selling, Grammy award winning, artist Nelly, AND working with Russell Simmons' Hip-Hop Summit Action Network, and many more to help at risk youth.

A father, and the Managing Editor of The Dallas Weekly, Dallas/ Fort Worth's #1 urban newspaper and media source where he is also a the founder of the newspapers' hip-hop section, interviewing and working such hip-hop artists, as Bun B, Rick Ross, actor/ director, Ice T, and Kendrick Lamar to name a few. Jihad is also a hip-hop content writer for The CW Television network, a contributing writer for The Final Call Newspaper, and a proud member of Muhammad Mosque No. 48 in Dallas, TX.

Rodney 'Asaad' Muhammad, a son, husband, father and Registered Member of The Nation of Islam under the guidance of The Honorable Minister Louis Farrakhan, who loves helping others achieve what they view as success.

A 4th Degree Black Belt in B.K.F. Fist Law under Sijo Saabir (Steve 'Sanders') Muhammad and a lover of knowledge, wisdom and understanding.

Rodney 'Asaad' Muhammad is a nationally known speaker, trainer and mentor. He brings fresh, innovative ideas to help you reach your goals.

Rodney has over 27 years of displayed courage and action in the business world. He has combined his years of speaking, training and mentoring into several audio programs and live trainings that are assisting people all over the world in achieving the results they desire using enlightening strategies.

www.MeetTheGoal.com

J. Cole meets Jihad H. Muhammad of Dynasty Hip-Hop Mentoring Program

Kendrick Lamar meets with Jihad H. Muhammad of Dynasty Hip-Hop Mentoring

Inspired by the work of The Hon. Min. Louis Farrakhan

GETTING YOUTH OFF THE STREETS WITH HIP-HOP

Stopping Youth Violence with Beats, Rhymes and music

Rick Ross meets with Jihad H Muhammad

Sign Up For FREE STUDIO TIME while slots last

Tech N9ne meets Jihad H Muhammad

Youth from Dynasty win $500 and meet with 4 Time Grammy award winner Erykah Badu

Jihad H Muhammad with J Kruz and B Kamp on air @ 97.9 The Beat

James W. Muhammad of Dynasty, introduces youth to platinum selling producers for opportunity

CW33 KDAF-TV

The **Dallas Weekly**

We work closely with these media outlets that represent the best in DFW's radio, TV, and newspaper markets

Hip-Hop ARTISTS, PRODUCERS, WRITERS, DANCERS, SINGERS, AGES 13-24, AS YOU CAN SEE WE CONNECT YOU TO THE INDUSTRY, CALL TO GET YOUR OPPORTUNITY

214-519-9016   314-243-4722

Sessions Weds. and Sun.

2429 Martin Luther King Jr. Blvd. Dallas, TX 75215

P.O. Box 18382, Phoenix, AZ 85005-8382

Bring America's Most-Booked
Teacher and Student Coach to Your School!

The C⦿urage Coach™

The Courage You Need,
To Live The Life You Deserve!

Parents
Teachers
Children

www.MeetTheGoal.com

Ask About
A Multi-School
Discount

The Courage Coach

BookTheCoach@MeetTheGoal.com
(731) 43-COACH

**Improve student morale, test scores,
and total school climate. End bullying today!**

Parents   Teachers   Children

The Final Call
ONLINE STORE

CDPACK LOSING-2

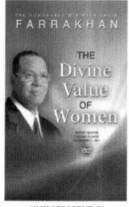

HLF110911DVD-2

CDPACKBLKWOMAN-2

CDPACK-PROTECT-2

CDPACKMARRIAGE-2

http://Store.FinalCall.com/   "Invest In Knowledge"
Customer Service (773) 602-1230 Ext. 200

The Brother Marcus and Sister Cecelia Show!

Featuring Singles Success Seminars and Marriage Empowerment Workshops!

Webinar and Interactive Chat Room Option:
www.startmeeting.com/wall/644-850-753

Conference Call Only: The Conference Call telephone number is (530) 881-1212. When prompted, enter the meeting ID, 644-850-753#

Every Sunday at 8:00 p.m. EST

 ## Wall, "the Protecting Friends" Marriage Counseling Services

Specializing in all Personal, Pre - Engagement, Courtship, Remarriage and Divorce and all other Marital Problems, Issues and Disputes - The only side we are on is the side of the Truth!

100% Confidentiality / You will never hear your personal business in the streets.....

* 20 Years Experience!
* Bible and Holy Qur'an Based Instruction from the Teachings of T.M.H.E.M. with the understanding of T.H.M.L.F.

Visit our Website at:
www.marcusandcecelia.com
or call 404-542-3808 to set up your appointment today!

All Love Offerings & Donations Accepted...

Your Service Providers,
Brother Marcus and Sister Cecelia

Brothers Jihad and Rodney are available for keynote presentations and for inspirational / educational relationship talks customized to your organization, or conference agenda.

Areas of Availability: Jihad is based in Dallas, Texas, and Rodney is based in Phoenix, Arizona and they are available nationally and worldwide. Contact us at (323) 533-6132 for information on how to bring us in to inspire better marriages in your city.

APPENDIX

Courting – The Right and Wrong Way to Start

1. Courtship: What do you know of another on first sight? It should first of all be time in which you are learning about the other person and in the process more about yourself. The devil puts more emphasis on "wooing" and far too less on knowledge. His definitions are immature and serve his evil aims and purposes. You both are gathering data on which to make a serious decision. A major key in that which makes for success is that both people must put forth their best effort to communicate honestly. Self-honesty is critical.

2. You are exploring each other's minds and hearts [to the extent that you can, as it is easier to see into the mind than the heart] and learning each other's motivations and aspirations; on how much do you agree and in what areas—both vital and not critical. You must also learn of those areas wherein you disagree too. There must be recognition that there will be more to learn of each other after marriage occurs—if it occurs.

3. The Honorable Elijah Muhammad said that agreement is the basis of love. The courting period shouldn't take years, but how long it takes depends on the quality of communication. For those who have an idea of what they want in as a mate they can come to a decision more rapidly. For others it may take longer. Much of this depends on how well each really knows themselves. Can one be true to themselves while ignorant of self?

4. The length of time to court also depends on the emotional maturity. The amount of time involved in the process does not necessarily reflect the intelligence and/or emotional maturity of

the participants in the process. However, courtship shouldn't last years and years—as Min. Farrakhan said, "long courtships are of no value." On the other hand if the courtship is settled on two or three days and marriage takes place at once, that marriage may last about that long. Smile.

5. How well do you know yourself? Self-knowledge provides the basis on which to make such a serious and proper decision. One's self concept is also tied inextricably to one's true concept of God. One's God is He on Whom we ultimately try to pattern oneself after---as whom you follow leads to your God.

6. Of the characteristics one should look for; first, a) is this person a Muslim. Why should you not want to consider a Muslim to marry? So, is the person you are considering a Muslim? You should know what a Muslim is yourself. Next, who is God and what does God want? From Allah come each other's rights, privileges and duties and obligations.

7. During the courtship period, there must be a respectful investigation of the other person's health; background, etc. what is the degree of your mutual compatibility—the simple definition of which is: 1 a) capable of living together harmoniously or getting along well together (with) b) in agreement; congruent (with); 2) that can work together, get along well together, combine well.

8. Friendship must first develop. See Surah 5:54-55 and 19:96. Allah desires that the Believers be friends of one another. Does not Minister Farrakhan teach this day and night? If you aren't friends first, you won't get married or if you do, it will not last long!

The preceding was Excerpted from: The Comprehensive Courtship Manual Volume 1, PRESENTED AT THE 3ᴿᴰ ANNUAL SINGLE'S RETREAT - AUGUST 17-20, 2006

Haziqah Safiyah Muhammad
February 28, 1974 - March 10, 2014

Testimonials for Tonja

"To Allah do I submit and seek refuge: My condolences to my brother Rodney 'Asaad' Muhammad on the loss of his wife and our sister Tonja Muhammad. I am really shocked and don't know the details but it is barely believable. Sis Tonja reached out to me once to point out to me some mistakes in the newspaper (Final Call). I said jokingly something like, "sister you need stop pointing out the mistakes in the newspaper and read the paper before it comes out!" She did. I started sending my columns and editorials to her before the paper went to press and she would correct mistakes before the newspaper came out. A great sister, a great help to our Nation, may Allah be pleased with her."
Brother Richard Muhammad (Managing Editor of The Final Call Newspaper)

Halif Khalif Khalifah says: "Yes Sir Brother Richard, Sister Tonja edited the First Edition of my book, "Melanin, Conscious Attunement...." while still at HU (Howard University). She worked part time in UBUS Books & Things. She was like a bright light in a dark place. I have plenty of remembrances of her from 18-22...never to be forgotten..."

"I first met Sister Tonja Muhammad at Muhammad Mosque #32, when Brother Rodney Asaad Muhammad, her husband introduced us, when they moved to Phoenix. She was very pleasant with a wonderful spirit. From the onset, she and her daughter Madinah, would be at the Wed. and Fri. Study Group Class, just about every week. She would give insightful comments during the discussion. She was not the type to sit back and not participate. Sister Tonja was so loved, in such a short time of being with us only 8 months, that she mad an indelible impact of dedication and service, which is worthy of emulation. Sister Tonja was sought after, not only by me to help as administrative assistant for the student ministry class, but also, Brother Student Secretary Stanley had recruited her on secretary staff. We are constantly looking for more brothers and sister with the same kind of work ethic and spirit as Sister Tonja Muhammad.
May Allah be pleased with her service and sacrifice."

As-Salaam Alaikum
Brother Charles Muhammad
Student Minister Muhammad Mosque No. 32, Phoenix, AZ.

Tonja Rene Muhammad
August 15, 1973 - April 8, 2014

33781350R00051

Made in the USA
Lexington, KY
09 July 2014